OLYMPIA

WARRIOR ATHLETES OF ANCIENT GREECE

ILLUSTRATIONS BY

DAVID KENNETT

TEXT BY DYAN BLACKLOCK

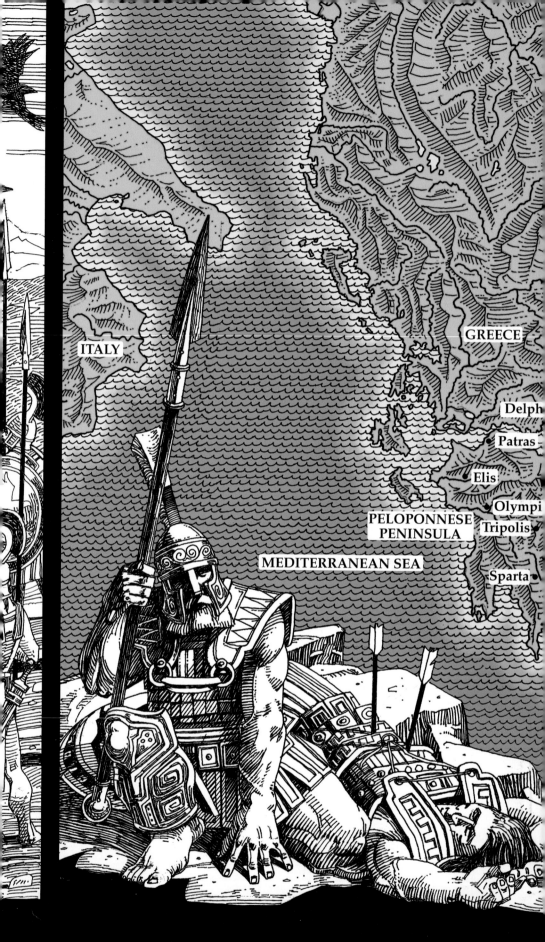

ITALY

GREECE

Delph

Patras

Elis

Olympi

PELOPONNESE
PENINSULA
Tripolis

MEDITERRANEAN SEA

Sparta

e eighth century B.C., was at war, not with other countries but

mountains of Greece divided the country into small city-states

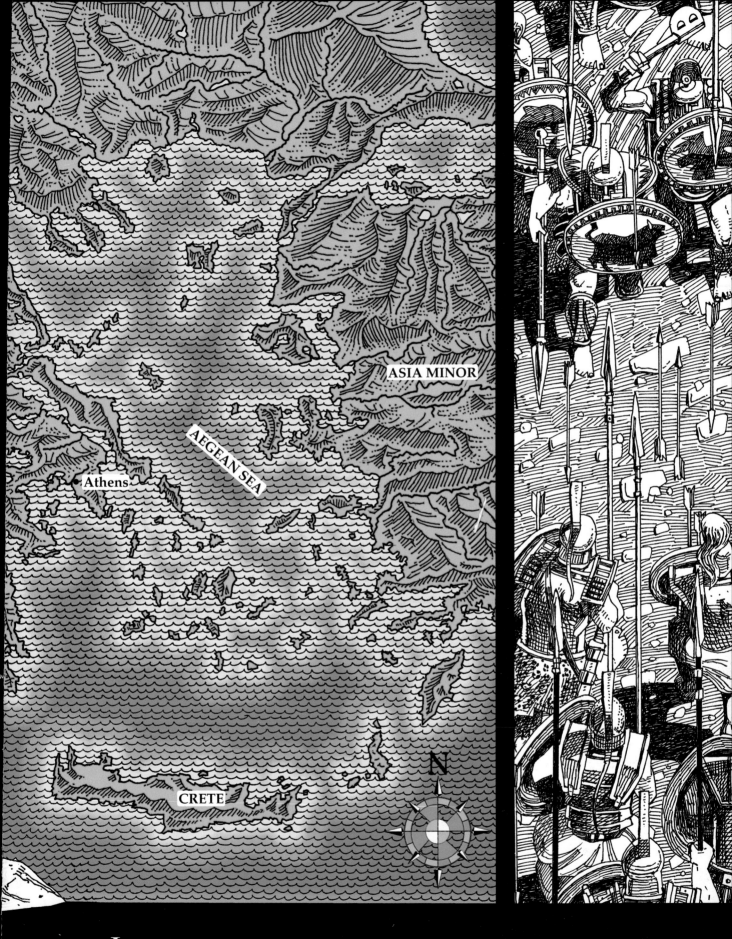

ASIA MINOR

AEGEAN SEA

Athens

CRETE

N

Although the Greek people believed in the same gods and the same religious places, their loyalty to their city was more important than their loyalty to other people of Greece. All over the country, neighbor fought neighbor.

After the killing came sickness and disease, but still the Greeks fought on.
It seemed the carnage would never stop.

In Elis, a city-state in the northwest part of Greece's Peloponnese Peninsula, King Iphitus watched in despair as his country tore itself apart. Iphitus felt certain there was a way to bring peace. He decided to consult the Oracle at Delphi.

The Oracle was thought to know the will of the gods. Speaking through an interpreter, she told Iphitus to go back to Elis and host an athletic competition open to all Greeks. It would be a way to stop the fighting for a while and bring people together in a competitive but peaceful activity.

Iphitus wasted no time. As soon as he returned to Elis he announced his intention to hold the games. Messengers were sent out all over Greece to cry out the news in every town marketplace.

Greek men ready for war were fit and athletic. They were proud of their bodies and of their strength. Athletic games gave them the opportunity to practice their skills away from the battlefield.

All events related to warfare. Chariot-racing, boxing, javelin, running, wrestling, and the *pankration* all developed skills that made men better soldiers. They competed naked to show off their superior physical condition. The Greeks believed it pleased their gods to watch the competitions.

All sporting competitions honored the gods and had to be held on sacred ground. Iphitus chose Olympia, a place where the greatest of gods, Zeus, had struck an olive tree with his thunderbolt. There had been a temple to Zeus on the site for hundreds of years.

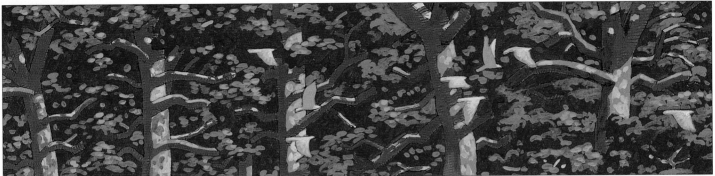

There was also a long history of games at Olympia—five brothers were said to have run a race here in 1500 B.C. Iphitus built an altar in two parts: a platform for the sacrifice and a mound of the ashes from the sacrificed animals. The altar, and later all sacred buildings, was built inside a beautiful grove of trees called the Altis.

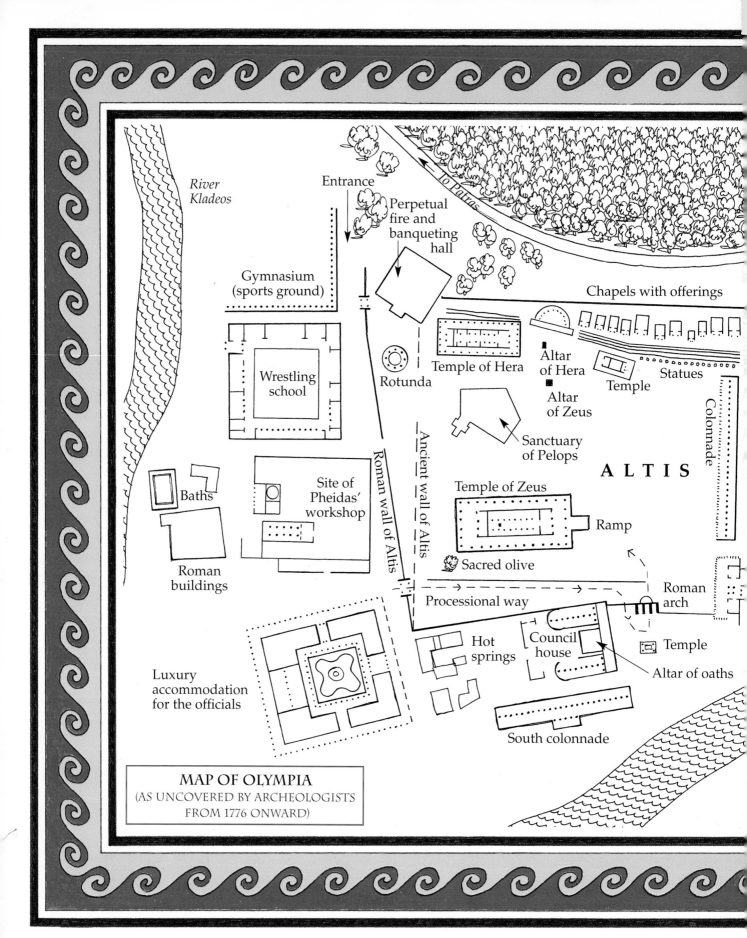

River
Kladeos

Entrance

Perpetual
fire and
banqueting
hall

To Patras

Chapels with offerings

Gymnasium
(sports ground)

Rotunda

Temple of Hera

Altar
of Hera

Altar
of Zeus

Temple

Statues

Wrestling
school

Sanctuary
of Pelops

ALTIS

Colonnade

Baths

Site of
Pheidas'
workshop

Roman wall of Altis

Ancient wall of Altis

Temple of Zeus

Ramp

Roman
buildings

Sacred olive

Processional way

Roman
arch

Luxury
accommodation
for the officials

Hot
springs

Council
house

Temple

Altar of oaths

South colonnade

MAP OF OLYMPIA
(AS UNCOVERED BY ARCHEOLOGISTS
FROM 1776 ONWARD)

Olympia had been a sacred place for hundreds of years before Iphitus held
his games. There were many stories and religious cults associated with the site.
There was enough flat ground between the two rivers bordering the site to hold
running races and horse races, as well as to house temples and altars.

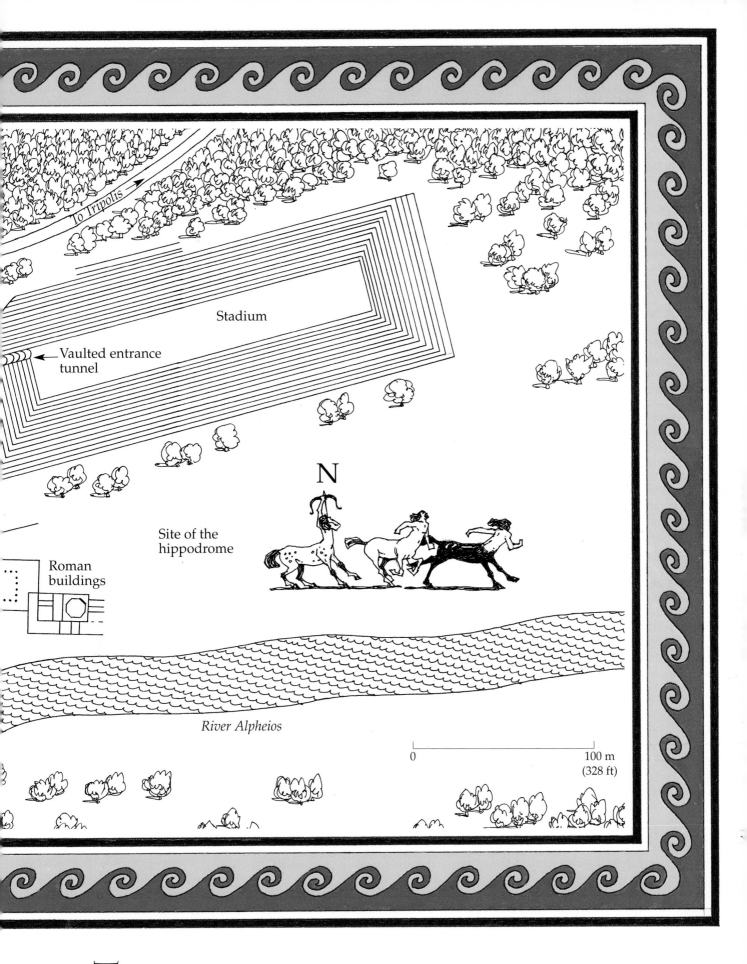

To Tripolis

Stadium

Vaulted entrance
tunnel

N

Site of the
hippodrome

Roman
buildings

River Alpheios

0   100 m
(328 ft)

The simple games begun by King Iphitus grew in size and reputation. Over the next few centuries the site was further developed and new sports were included in the competition. Buildings were added, statues put up, walls built, and amenities improved. Many rulers of Greece left their mark on Olympia.

From the time that Iphitus reintroduced the athletic competition, the games were well attended. Although the site was in a remote part of the country, the roads that led to Olympia quickly filled as spectators made their way there from all over Greece.

A sacred truce was declared throughout the country to give people the chance to travel safely. Kings, jugglers, rich men, and traders of all kinds crowded the roads.

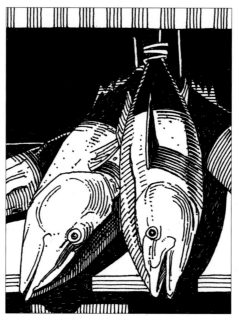

The Altis quickly filled with beautiful rainbow colors as traders set up their tents. Food sellers and hawkers shouted their wares as the crowds milled about. Visitors to Olympia left offerings to the gods of pots, shields, statues, and other beautiful things.

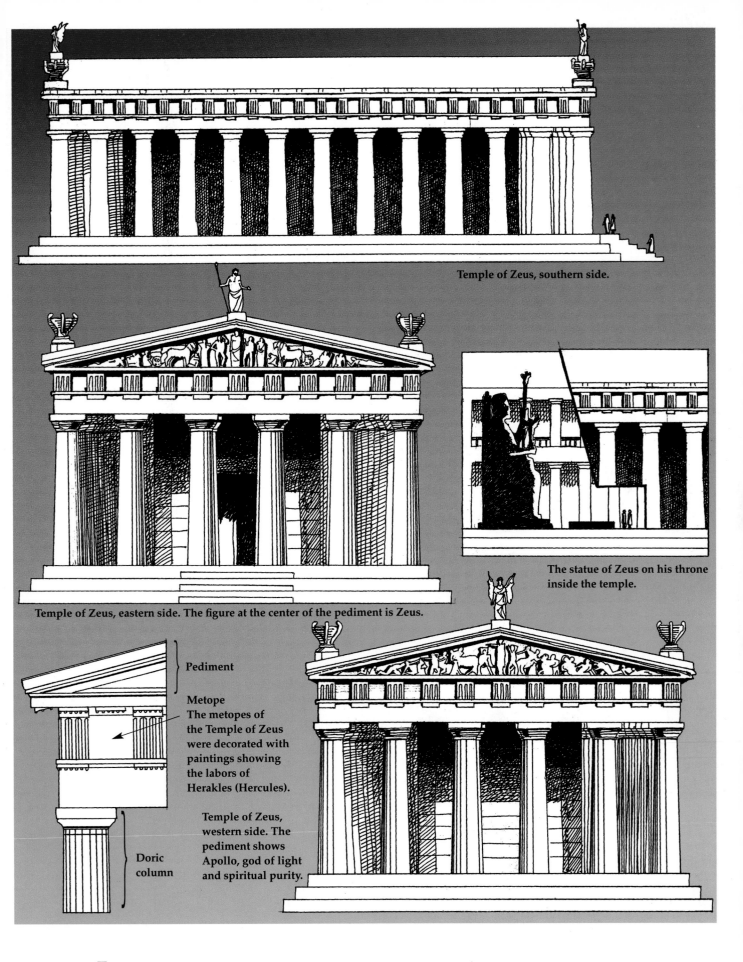

Temple of Zeus, southern side.

The statue of Zeus on his throne inside the temple.

Temple of Zeus, eastern side. The figure at the center of the pediment is Zeus.

Pediment

Metope
The metopes of the Temple of Zeus were decorated with paintings showing the labors of Herakles (Hercules).

Doric column

Temple of Zeus, western side. The pediment shows Apollo, god of light and spiritual purity.

A new temple to Zeus was built in the fifth century B.C. It housed one of the seven wonders of the ancient world, a statue of the god Zeus seated on his throne made by the sculptor Pheidas.

Made entirely of ivory and gold, by methods no modern sculptor can replicate, the statue of Zeus was like a piece of jewelry. Forty-three feet (13m) high, it was created in pieces over a wooden framework and could be dismantled. At the feet was a pool of olive oil, which cast a reflective glow on the statue.

Such a large statue made of bronze or stone would have looked hard and stiff.
The ivory and gold, softened by reflected light, made the face of Zeus look real.

There was a four-year gap between games and much to prepare at the site each time. Roads, wells, camping areas, and temples had to be made ready. This work was overseen by the *hellanodikai*, purple-robed officials who also acted as judges. Slaves, non-Greeks, women, the overweight, and the unfit were disqualified from competing. Married women were forbidden even to attend.

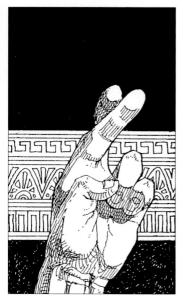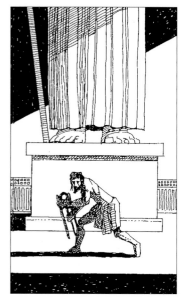

Murderers, or anyone who had broken the sacred truce or sinned against the gods by stealing from a sacred place, were also disqualified. At that time there were no documents to prove a person's identity. Contestants had to swear on the entrails of a boar that they were who they claimed to be. *Hellanodikai* kept all records.

Since the games honored the gods, there were ceremonies, purification rituals, and animal sacrifices. The first day of what became a five-day festival began with such ceremonies. Additionally, the *hellanodikai* conducted a lottery to see which athletes would compete against each other. There was also a contest to find the best trumpeter. The winner would announce each event.

Boys' events, which included running, wrestling, boxing, and, for a time, the *pankration* and the pentathlon, were held in the afternoon of the first day. These events were held in the stadium. Occasionally the *hellanodikai* decided a boy was too big for these events and forced him to compete with the men instead.

All horse-related events were held on the second day. Chariot-racing took place in the hippodrome at sunrise. It was one of the oldest and most popular events. Teams of horses pulled chariots around a dangerous course where accidents were common.

24

Slaves were used as charioteers, and the winner was the owner, not the driver. Only the very wealthy could afford to bring a chariot team all the way to Olympia. Even today, horse racing is known as "the sport of kings."

The most dangerous point on the chariot course was the *taraxippus*, or "terror of horses." Just before the turn a rider needed to stay as close as possible to the turning post without catching the hub of the wheel on the post.

At the same time he had to urge on the outside horses and rein in the inside horses. To complicate matters, the rising sun blinded drivers. There were many spectacular spills as drivers competed to be first around the turn.

The area surrounding the hippodrome contained open-air restaurants and many kinds of stalls. Food sellers, traders, entertainers, and probably thieves, exploited the crowd between events.

In the equestrian events there were many heats to decide who would
compete for the crown of olive branches that would be awarded to the winner.
Only highly skilled riders could compete in these events.

The riders in the equestrian events did not use saddles. Riding bareback,
they used the pressure of their thighs on the horses' flanks to urge the horses on.

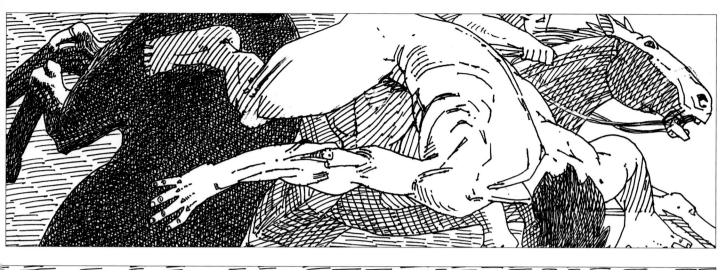

Whips and simple bridles provided the only other means of controlling the horses. When accidents occurred they created problems for other horses and riders.

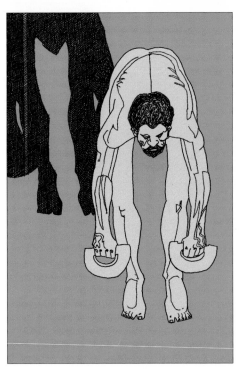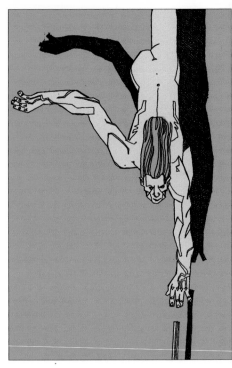

The pentathlon was held in the afternoon of the second day. This consisted of five different events—discus, jumping, javelin, running races, and wrestling, in that order. In the jumping event, the athletes used stone weights to help propel themselves forward.

Athletes who competed in the pentathlon were lighter than other wrestlers, and so they needed a greater degree of skill and agility to win this event. The pentathlon events were very popular, and drew big crowds.

The third day began with religious ceremonies that continued through the morning. A hundred cattle were ritually slaughtered and their legs burned on the altar as an offering to Zeus. The remaining flesh was used for the feast later that evening. Competitors and spectators alike conducted sacrifices to honor the gods.

The foot races, held after lunch on the third day, included three types of events: the *stade* (one length of the stadium, or 630 feet [192 m]), the *diaulos* (two lengths) and the *dolichos* (24 lengths, or about 2.9 miles[4.6 km]). A jump-start was punishable by a public flogging administered by the *hellanodikai*. In the evening there was a great feast to celebrate the games and the gods.

The wrestling competition was held on the fourth day. It was one of the most popular sports. Wrestlers used their strength to try to throw their opponent to the ground three times, from a standing position. Most of the holds are still used today. In order to get a better grip, wrestlers rubbed their bodies with oil and threw sand over themselves.

The *pankration*, which followed the wrestling, was the most violent of sports. There were only two rules—no biting and no eye-gouging—but dislocated limbs, fingers, and heels were common. Contestants stuffed sand in each other's mouths, kicked, trampled, and used strangleholds. The event continued until one of the athletes signaled defeat.

Boxing originated in Sparta, the most warlike of the Greek city-states. It was intended to teach a man how to ward off blows to the head. Oiled strips of leather protected the hands. Matches were not point-scored, nor did they take place inside a ring. As with the *pankration*, the match continued until one boxer signaled defeat or was unable to continue.

A boxing match could go on for hours. A boxer was allowed to drop to one knee during a match if he needed a short rest. In a match where there was no clear winner, contestants agreed to undefended blows to settle it. Such fierce blows sometimes resulted in death.

The fourth day ended with the hoplite race. Hoplites were the heavy infantry in Greek armies. In battle they stood shoulder to shoulder and raised their shields in a formation known as the hoplite phalanx. The ability of Greek soldiers to run fully armed was one of their great strengths in battle.

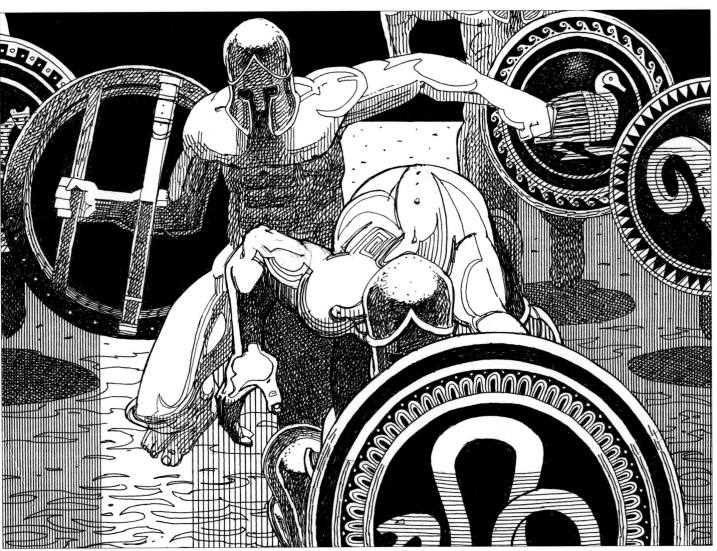

The hoplite race was originally a running race where men wore helmets and greaves and carried shields. Eventually the competitors ran only with heavy shields. To make the race fair, the *hellanodikai* kept specially made shields in the temple of Zeus.

The fifth day was the last day of the games. At dawn a young boy of noble family used a golden sickle to cut branches from the sacred olive tree in the Altis. These were made into wreaths, with which the *hellanodikai* crowned the winners.

The olive tree symbolized long life, and was considered to be a gift from the gods. The crowning ceremony was a moment of great religious significance. It was followed by other ceremonies and animal sacrifices to thank the gods for the games.

The games concluded with a feast. All who attended celebrated the end of the games. The long journey home was still ahead of them, but for now they played music, told stories, and discussed the most extraordinary events of the past week.

The last games were held at Olympia in 393 A.D. By this time, winning
had become more important than honoring the gods. Professional
sportsmen sought personal glory and financial rewards. Under the later rule
of the Romans, all Greek festivals considered to be pagan were banned.

The Visigoths also invaded Greece and destroyed many of the temples at Olympia. After the Visigoths came the Vandals, who destroyed even more of the ancient site of the games. Later still, earthquakes and floods changed the site forever.

In spite of its many invaders, Olympia was not completely destroyed. The barbarian hordes that ransacked Olympia threw many significant objects down wells, inadvertently preserving them. The site was rediscovered in 1766, and archaeologists conducted many excavations after that. Those discoveries inspired the modern Olympic Games which began in 1896.

GLOSSARY

barbarian • member of a primitive tribe.

city-state • a city and its surrounding territory, forming a separate state.

discus • heavy disc, thick in the middle, thrown in Olympic events.

equestrian events • horse-riding events.

greaves • armor to protect the shins.

hawkers • traveling sellers of goods.

hippodrome • course for chariot races.

hoplites • heavily armed foot soldiers.

jump-start • false start; a break from the starting line before the signal.

Oracle • priest or priestess who gives advice from the gods.

pankration • savage, ancient Greek sports event that combined boxing and wrestling.

pediment • triangular front part of a building.

pentathlon • athletic event comprising five separate events for each competitor.

phalanx • body of foot soldiers drawn in close together.

purification rituals • religious ceremonies for cleansing.

ritual games • games to honor the gods.

seven wonders of the world • seven buildings or monuments of the ancient world regarded as extraordinary.

sickle • farming tool with a semicircular blade, used for cutting.

stranglehold • hold that gives a wrestler complete control of his opponent.

Vandals • tribe of the fourth and fifth centuries CE that ravaged Mediterranean countries, destroying books and art.

Visigoths • West Goths, a branch of the Goths, a barbarian tribe.

wreath • a ring of branches worn as a crown.

Zeus • king of the Greek gods.

For my littlest warrior, Joe—D. B.

For Daiman: Thanks—D. K.

David Kennett used fineliner pen on bond paper and acrylic paint on systems board for the illustrations in this book.
Carol McLean-Carr applied background color digitally to some black-and-white artwork.

INDEX

Text copyright © 2000 by Dyan Blacklock
Illustration copyright © 2000 by David Kennett

First published in the United States of America in 2001 by Walker Publishing Company, Inc.

Published simultaneously in Canada by Fitzhenry and Whiteside, Markham, Ontario L3R 4T8

Originally published in Australia in 2000 by Scholastic Australia

Library of Congress Cataloging-in-Publication Data

Kennett, David, 1959-
  Olympia : warrior athletes of Ancient Greece/
  illustrations by David Kennett ; text by Dyan Blacklock.
    p. cm.
  Originally published: Norwood, S. Aust. : Omnibus Books, 2000.
  Includes index.
  ISBN 0-8027-8790-8 (hardcover) -- ISBN 0-8027-8791-6 (lib. bdg.)
  1. Olympic games (Ancient)--Juvenile literature. [1. Olympic games (Ancient)] I. Blacklock, Dyan. II. Title.

GV23 .K45 2001
796.48'0938--dc21

Printed in Singapore
10 9 8 7 6 5 4 3 2 1

2001023553